013

FOR EMICY

Bonnie fenn

Sharai Platt

In loving memory of my aunt, Gertrude Mitchell,
whose eyes danced with pride each time she whispered,
"Oh Sweetheart, you can do anything."
What a gift it was to have been loved like that!

This story is dedicated to my first grandchild, Kayleigh.
Her presence in my life creates a warm and constant invitation
to once again visit childhood.
I now whisper to her,
"My Little Honeybunch, you can do anything."
What a gift it is, to love like this!

Wallaby
The Wannabe

Written By
Bonnie Feuer

Illustrated by
Sharai Platt

THE
CONNECTICUT PRESS

Monroe, CT

Inquiries should be addressed to:
The Connecticut Press
135 Church Street
Monroe, CT 06468
www.connecticutpress.com

Library of Congress Cataloguing-in-Publication Data

Feuer, Bonnie
    Wallaby The Wannabe
Includes illustrations by Sharai Platt
ISBN 978-0-9825468-7-1 (hard cover edition)   Library of Congress Control Number: 2011960813

1. Children's literature   2. Animals - Fiction   3. Australia   4. Wallabies

MADE IN

Wallaby's eyes popped open. Curled up safely in Mom's pouch, she yawned and stretched her legs. She peeked outside. It was nighttime in Australia and Wallaby was wide awake. No more resting for me, she thought. "I want to see everything."

Wallaby pushed down on her feet... then jumped out of Mom's pouch onto the soft, damp grass.

Blinking in the darkness, she took one small hop...
then another... and another, and Wallaby was on her way.

Mom followed quietly, not too far behind.

J umping and hopping through the last bit of night time, Wallaby came upon many trees. The forest was alive with noise. Whoops and calls and shrieks and chattering went on all at the same time.

Wallaby stood still, listening and looking. From the corner of her eye, she saw two bright red spots against a tree. They seemed to glow in the darkness. She hopped over to get a closer look. There, stuck to the tree trunk, was a colorful new friend with gigantic red eyes.

"Hi," Wallaby said. "It's cool the way you stick to that tree!"

"Thank you for the compliment," answered the new friend. "I am a red-eyed tree frog. My feet have tiny suction cups. I can stick to anything and I stay awake all night doing just that."

"That's great!" exclaimed Wallaby.

"I love your bright colors and giant red eyes.

How you cling to that tree

and your very small size.

When you don't want to stick,

you can jump far and long,

and your musical chirping

is almost a song.

I wanna be a tree frog like you,

To shine in the dark; neon, red, green, and blue."

Not far behind... Mom smiled.

Wallaby said "good night" to the tree frog and hopped on her way. Leaving the noisy forest, she jumped along easily on Australia's flat, dry plains. It was almost dawn, when to her left Wallaby heard an odd sound. It seemed like a beating drum. She turned and hopped closer. As the drumming got louder, the strangest thing happened. Right in front of Wallaby's eyes, in a space that was empty just a second ago, stood a tall and fluffy new friend.

"How do you do?" asked Wallaby. "It's amazing the way your feathers blend in with the plains. I almost jumped right past you."

"Thank you very much," smiled the new friend. "I am an emu; one of the largest birds in the land. My feathers get lighter and darker depending on where I go. It is called camouflage and it keeps me safe."

"How wonderful," answered Wallaby.

"Your drumming voice makes an interesting sound.

It thuds and it rumbles as you run around.

Your feathers can turn from dark brown to light

as camouflage helps you to hide in plain sight.

An emu is all I wanna be.

So tall and so proud on the plains... running free."

Very quietly... Mom chuckled.

The emu waved a heavy wing and left Wallaby standing there...

thinking.

As an orange sun rose over the horizon, Wallaby was once again on her way. She jumped and hopped then finally decided to rest. Rocking back on her strong tail, Wallaby looked up at an early morning sky streaked with yellow and red. She breathed deeply and the scent of sweet spice reached her nose.

She hopped in the direction of that delicious aroma. Soon, Wallaby found herself among many trees that smelled so good.

A few feet above her, leaves rustled. Wallaby looked up. Sleeping on a thick branch with her baby was an adorable new friend.

"Excuse me," whispered Wallaby. "I'm sorry to wake you, but you're so cute. I would like to meet you."

The new friend yawned and shifted her baby onto her back. "Thank you for your kind words," she said softly. "I am a koala. I sleep all day in these eucalyptus trees and eat the leaves at night. They are so full of water that I never, ever need a drink. My name actually means, 'no drink.'"

"Wow," breathed Wallaby.

"You look like a bear sleeping up there,

And your gray and white fur is like beautiful hair.

There's such a cute smile beneath your black nose,

and your baby is clutching your back with its toes.

A koala is what I wanna-be, a cuddly bear asleep

in a tree."

Not very far away… Mom grinned. The eyes of the tired koala started to droop, so Wallaby hopped away. All of that talk about water made Wallaby thirsty. She jumped along, hoping to find a river or stream.

It was a peaceful and quiet time until all of a sudden, came a cackling noise. Wallaby stopped to listen, thinking that nearby some-one must be laughing. There, straight ahead, was a tree with a hole in it. The laughter was coming from that hole.

Wallaby smiled at the happy sound and jumped towards it. "Hello in there!" shouted Wallaby. "You sound like fun."

Out of the hole, popped a chubby bird. "Thank you for your kind-ness," chirped the new friend. "I am a kookaburra and in this hole is my nest. It is inside this homey tree trunk that my babies will hatch from eggs."

Hee Hee
Hee Hee

"How cozy," said Wallaby.

"A happy bird with a belly so white,

and royal blue wings to help you in flight.

Your home is a hole in a tree where you nest.

Your call is more charming than all of the rest.

A kookaburra is what I wanna be.

I believe that your stripe

would look perfect on me."

Not too far behind, Mom just shook
her head.

Wallaby remembered that she needed a drink, so she said "goodbye" to her new friend and jumped away, listening for the sound of water.

She took very long leaps, needing to quickly find a stream. It was almost dusk and in between the trees the sun was getting lower.

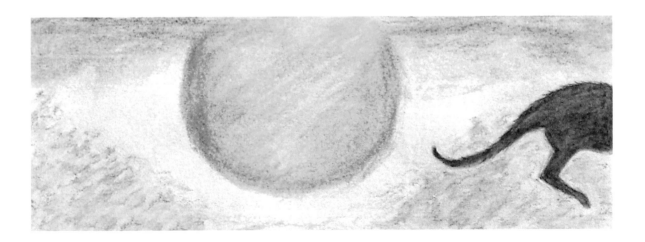

Finally, the trees parted and a river-
bank came into view. Wallaby hurried
to its edge.

Getting ready to take a drink, she saw something rise up and slap the surface of the river. Wallaby jumped back!

Silently, she watched as an unusual face appeared and disappeared. It seemed to be a duck, but it was covered with dark fur. Wallaby tried to talk to the new friend, but it kept diving and paddling.

"Hello," called Wallaby. "You're a great swimmer."

The new friend stopped in the middle of a dive and answered, "Well hi, and thank you for the compliment. I am a platypus, and I swim for most of the day. My tail is like a boat rudder, sending me quickly through the river."

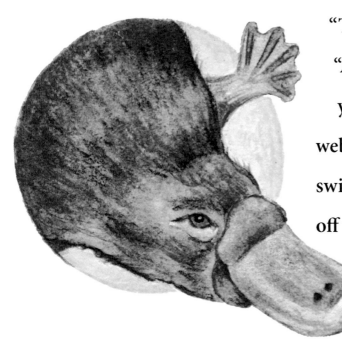

"That's terrific," said Wallaby. "A bill like a duck, and I see you've laid eggs. There are webs on the feet of your strong swimming legs. The water rolls off you to help you get dry, and though you've been friendly, you're really quite shy.

My wish is to swim and dive as you do. I wanna be a platypus, too."

Near by… Mom laughed right out loud. Wallaby turned and saw her as the shy platypus swam away.

"I didn't know you were here," Wallaby said.

"Oh, I've been right behind you all along," answered Mom.

"You're too little to be out by yourself. I am with you to make sure you stay safe.

"Now, I have something to show you. Go back to the edge of the river and take that drink." Wallaby did as she was told and bent over to sip the water. It was so clear; you could almost see the river bottom.

As she lowered her head, Wallaby saw someone looking back at her. She squinted her eyes and moved closer. The friend moved closer.

"Hi," said Wallaby. "Your face is as sweet as a baby deer." This new friend did not answer. "Hello," repeated Wallaby a little louder, "I love your giant tail." There was still no answer.

"Listen," explained Mom, "That new friend can't answer because that new friend is you. You are a wallaby, and what you see is your own reflection. We can all see ourselves in clear water."

"Me!" exclaimed Wallaby.

"I love my gray color and very kind face.

With my sturdy hind legs, I can win any race.

Someday in my pouch, a baby will sleep.

My large springy tail helps me balance and leap.

A wallaby is what I wanna be.

I love every part of me that I see!"

Mom nodded and said...

"All creatures are different,

some have fur,

some have wings,

one makes drumming noises while another one sings.

They might stick to a tree, or wiggle or swim.

They could carry their baby, or sleep on a limb.

It's great to be different.

It can help you go far.

Just take a close look and see all that you are."

Standing close to Mom, Wallaby smiled.

Glossary

aroma   A long lasting, enticing smell.

emu   A large, flightless Australian bird related to the ostrich.

eucalyptus leaf   A leaf that is filled with an oily, watery substance, which is all that Koalas eat.

koala   An Australian marsupial that has thick gray fur and large ears.

kookaburra   A bird of southern Australia having brown, white and blue feathers. Its call resembles laughter.

plains   A clear, open, flat area of terrain.

platypus   An egg laying mammal having a broad flat tail, webbed feet, and a snout resembling a duck's bill. It lives on land and in water.

reflection   An exact image formed in water or certain types of glass.

tree frog   A nocturnal frog having a green color, blue highlights, and red eyes.

wallaby   An Australian animal that looks like a kangaroo, but is smaller.